Each Inner Workbook is a self-study retreat or workshop that you can do at home. They are designed to become a part of your day, just like that first cup of tea, and invite you to journal the experience as you develop your practice, making it your own.

Contents

Where to begin
04

How to Flow Journal
12

Create your intention
16

Going with the flow
24

The gift of time
32

Mindful. Kindful.
40

The still quiet voice within
48

Full stop
56

Creating rituals
64

Everything and anything
72

Endings and beginnings
76

> "In the *journal* I do not just *express myself* more openly than I could do to any person; *I create myself*"
>
> Susan Sontag

Where to *begin*

A trusted teacher once invited me to journal a letter from my future self to the woman I was then. I was in a difficult place in my life and had no idea what to write, but I picked up my pen and allowed the words to flow.

That piece of writing inspired a whole collection of love letters from a wiser me. And turned out to be one of the foundational steps for a powerful period of personal change.

Since then, I have journaled many hundreds, possibly thousands, of times. Sometimes writing beautiful things. Sometimes writing non sensical things. Sometimes writing about deeply challenging things. Sometimes writing about the most uplifting things.

The practice remains the same. But what I write changes every time.

For me, that is part of the incredible power of this beautiful work.

We are all of us ever-changing. Even when we feel most stuck, our thoughts and feelings shift endlessly, as we respond to our inner and outer worlds. Finding ways to understand, process, clarify and, crucially, be with what we're thinking, feeling and experiencing is an essential component of personal growth. Journaling gives us a way of disentangling what binds us; a way of moving forward.

But where do we begin?

Before writing that very first piece, I thought I understood what journaling was all about. But my belief was based on rules I'd learned at school, things I'd read about how journaling should be, and fears of getting it wrong.

Starting with a blank sheet of paper and a set of fixed ideas can feel so daunting. And can be the very things that stop us starting at all.

So, we begin with compassion. And that's really what being in the flow is about. Together, we'll explore how to access your wisest, kindest voice – deepening your self-awareness with profound self-compassion as we go.

I'll share journaling prompts, along with reflective questions, mindful moments and gentle guidance. There's also a series of recorded meditations for you to listen to, whenever you wish to sink a little further into your practice.

The mindfulness teacher Sharon Salzburg tells us we can always begin again. So whether journaling is completely new to you, or something you used to love and want to return to, or something you once tried but didn't enjoy at the time, I hope you find the practices I share useful for you.

I have been through periods in my life where I've journaled every day. And other times when I've barely written at all. Both are okay. I have come to see my journal as a place of sanctuary. A place of no judgement and no rules. Safe in the knowledge the whole of me is always welcome and I can always return, just as I am.

So. Where do we begin? We pick up our pen. And let the words flow.

Trust *the* process

There are many approaches to journaling, from bullet journaling, to diary writing, to drawing, to recording yourself speaking out loud. And they're all useful. There is no 'right' way to journal. It simply comes down to what you prefer.

The approach I recommend for this book (and my favourite route) is what I've come to call Flow Journaling – where you tap into your stream of consciousness. Over the years, I've developed my own practice, just as you will too. I share some of my hints and ideas with you throughout this workbook, so please pick up the ones you love and ignore the ones that don't feel right for you.

At its heart, Flow Journaling gives us an opportunity for free-flow expression. Just putting pen to paper and seeing what spills onto the page. It can include images as well as words, poetry and prose, questions and answers – everything is allowed.

One of the keys is to resist the urge to edit. Allow the words and meaning to fall onto the page in their raw form. This may mean broken grammar, jumping thoughts, nonsensical phrasing and moments of astonishing clarity – for me, that's the true spirit of Flow Journaling. Allowing what is. Scraps of words, half-considered thoughts, that's often how Flow Journaling works, so part of this process is learning to trust in the act of writing, rather than thinking about how or why or even what you're writing.

For me, the act of writing is a form of meditation. It is a time when everything else falls away; leaving just me, my pen, my journal - and whatever happens to fall onto the page.

In choosing to journal, you are creating a channel for things to begin to shift.

We can't always see what's happening – and in the moment it may not feel as though much is very different – but trust that deep in your subconscious, there is a process taking place.

What I find curious is how, after journaling, you can find you feel a sense of relief, as though you've been unburdened. Or you may feel as though you've found the answer to something. Or you could notice something feels much clearer to you – as if you've talked it through with a dear, wise friend... which, of course, you have.

Trusting the process also speaks to the importance of having a compassionate stance. If you find you are writing critically, or with harsh judgement – of yourself, of others, or about a situation – notice that's what's coming up and ask yourself, in the journal, how can I bring more compassion here?

Your inner, deeper, wisest, kindest Self will help you see the way.

Why journal?

A simple truth is: we can't write as fast as we think.

When we Flow Journal, our brain slows down. We find ourselves sinking beneath the layers of chattering thoughts, familiar patterns and long-held beliefs, revealing fresh insights and previously unseen wisdom.

Or not.

Which is fine, of course. We're not journaling 'for' something. We're simply journaling.

Always without judgement. Always with compassion for whatever arises.

The purpose is to allow yourself space to reflect and see what appears, trusting there's no right or wrong way to notice and record your own words. Your thoughts and feelings are yours to notice; to record however you wish. A space where you are completely free to say and think everything and anything.

I see it as the private writing of the soul – the truly personal place where there is only my voice, albeit I may notice many parts of me speaking. And while it can sometimes feel as though there is something else guiding my pen as I write, I know the questions, answers, challenges and encouragement are coming from within me – from my inner wisdom.

When something feels complex or hard or impossible to overcome, journaling is always there as a tool to support us in working through what we're noticing.

It can also help bring order to chaos, support us when we're feeling anxious or stressed and expands our thinking when we're feeling stuck or limited in some way. It enables us to understand our heart's desires – and keep sight of where we are heading. In short, it gives us a way to keep coming home to our deepest, wisest self.

What can *get* in *the* way?

As we commit to a practice, we begin to build the habit. We make connections in our brain that help us embed the behaviour, and each time we revisit the practice, those connections become clearer, stronger. But of course, like anything new, there can be things that get in the way.

We might think journaling is something we 'should' do, but we resist it – rarely, if ever, picking up our pen. Perhaps with a sense of, 'When I have some peace and quiet, then I'll journal', or 'When I'm feeling calmer, then I'll journal', or 'When I can take a break from work or family duties, then I'll journal'. Maybe telling ourselves we haven't got the time or head space to write 'properly' right now.

We might feel self-conscious about journaling, unsure of what others might think – maybe believing it's okay for them but not for the likes of us. We could be worried what we're writing is self-indulgent or meaningless, our inner critic telling us we can't write or there's no point trying; what if we have nothing to say?

Deeper down, we may worry about what the process could unlock inside us. Or feel shame at what others would think if they read what we wrote, so we edit our words in our mind.

Or we could simply feel the discomfort of unfamiliarity with a brand-new practice.

I've felt all these things. And more. They are all okay. They are all absolutely normal.

Just remember this is a tool to support you. You use it whatever way feels best for you – perhaps including exploring some of the thoughts you have about it. Learning to be with what comes up, trusting yourself, noticing and naming are all compassionate skills. And all part of the process.

The most important thing is that this is YOUR process – there's no right or wrong way to think about it or to do it. And there's certainly no shoulds about it.

How to *Flow* Journal

As I've already said, there are no rules here. Simply some gentle guidance you might find useful. I'll share some more later, but for now here are some great ideas to help you get started:

1 Before you begin: Find a space where you won't be disturbed. Switch off all distractions. If you've time and inclination, maybe get a warm drink and a blanket. Light a candle and scatter a few drops of essential oil. Scents of lavender, rosemary, orange or juniper all bring their own energy – some relaxing, others stimulating. Experiment to find ones you love, or create your own blend.

Make it a place you love. Get a pen you like using.

2 Once you've settled: Write. Keep the words flowing – even if you end up writing 'I don't know what to write', just keep going. We don't journal for an outcome, we simply journal.

3 Begin by writing the day's prompt: Put this at the top of your page – it's a lovely way of connecting with, and settling into the meaning each prompt holds for you.

4 It's up to you how long you write for: A page, two pages, 5 minutes, 20 minutes. Whatever works for you is good. Aim to have some consistency, at least initially. So, if you know you won't have time to journal for 20 minutes every day, set a pattern you'll find easier to repeat. I tend to write two pages, and that's what I've included for you in this book, but you can use the space however you wish.

5 Daily is useful but not essential: It takes patience and practice to build a new habit, so if you choose to write more or less one day, that's okay. It's all in your hands (literally).

6 When you get to the end of the page or your timer goes off… Stop: Close the journal and resist the urge to read over what you've written. You can always go back to it later, but for now let the words rest. They've done their work.

A couple of *thoughts*

When I was at school we had a very strict, very traditional English teacher. She was terrifying and brilliant in equal measure and I owe a lot to her – both in the rules she taught me and in how I ultimately learned to challenge those rules…

But the things we learn at the knees of our caregivers and educators can be incredibly deeply embedded. They can feel like unbreakable edicts, rather than just something another human once said.

So it is that we can find ourselves resisting the idea of letting go as we write. We want to make sure all the i's are dotted and the t's are crossed – because that's what we've been taught to do. But sometimes, with Flow Journaling, the words want to flow faster than we can keep up, and grammar and spelling and paragraphs and handwriting can all go out the window.

The act of writing becomes more important than how it looks or sounds.

Safely challenging the beliefs of our inner 'good child/good student' can become a wonderful part of this practice.

Lastly, the invitation is to consider whether or not you wish to date your journal entries.

It can feel useful. To have a sense of a point in time when you wrote a certain thing, when a certain feeling, experience, thought or belief was uppermost in your mind. So you can look back at some point in the future and maybe see what helped embed that thought, feeling or behaviour – or what helped release it.

Or you may prefer not to timestamp your writing at all. You may prefer to simply allow it to be what you wrote that day, without any attachment to knowing precisely when you wrote it.

Because, of course, if we find we're creating something in order to look back on it, we're sitting the activity simultaneously in the future and the past, rather than firmly in the present. It's something I'm mindful of for myself, and this may resonate with you too.

My own journal entries are simply labelled Day 1, 2, 3, and so on, all the way through to wherever I am now.

This approach helps remove any sense of judgement for missing a day, and it also stops each entry being fixed in a certain time. It's just a piece of writing that happened to fall from your pen. I see this approach as another beautiful way of releasing attachment to what we've written.

When I began to label entries in this way, I simply chose a day to begin and called it Day 1.

I managed to resist the urge to count back through previous journals to see how many 'days' I was really up to. And, since then, I've journaled in other books and not included them in my total count. It's a way to gently challenge the part of me that wants to prove how 'good' a journaler I am – everything is part of the practice.

If this appeals, even if you've been journaling for many years, perhaps see how it is to begin today with Day 1 and then go from there. You could even begin each new journal, or even each new entry, Day 1.

Now, let's begin...

Create *your* intention

Before picking up your pen, you may like to take a Mindful Moment to get settled and invite an intention to arise. Something to accompany you and help guide your way.

Mindful Moment
Begin with your posture. If you're in a chair, sit upright but not stiff, feet flat on the floor, hands resting lightly in your lap. Or if you prefer to be on the floor, fold your legs to create that sturdy triangular base to support yourself, perhaps with a small cushion beneath your bottom. Or you may prefer to lie down, maybe with a blanket pulled over you. Whatever posture you prefer, make yourself comfortable.

Allow your eyes to close and settle deeper into where you're sitting or lying.

Gently scan your body, seeing where you could bring a little more comfort, a little more ease. Learning how to look after our own needs is a wonderful compassion practice. This is a moment to really sink into where you are sitting or lying.

Notice the natural rhythm and pace of your breath. You're not trying to change anything. Simply noticing. Taking your time to be in this moment. And this one. And this one.

As you rest here, invite your intention to rise up within you.

How do you wish to feel as you move through this practice, exploring the writing that's to come?

If nothing arises immediately, that's okay, just imagine: if you knew how you wished to feel as you journal, what would that be? It may be a word, phrase or image that arises for you. Simply allow what is, and note it below.

_____

_____

_____

_____

_____

_____

 I have recorded each of the Mindful Moments in this journal as individual meditations you can listen to.

innerworkproject.com/product/
in-the-flow

Self-Reflection Check-In

What are you looking forward to from this process?
◊
Exploring a new way of journaling
◊
Revisiting/renewing the practice of journaling
◊
Trying journaling as a brand-new practice
◊
Seeing how it is to commit to journaling and build the habit

As I pick up my pen to write, I am noticing

How it feels to hold space for my Self

Today I feel...

Going *with* the *flow*

Now we're starting to get into our flow. And each time you return to the practice, the flow deepens. The first series of prompts has been about developing our ability to really notice what's coming up. Learning to pay mindful, kindful attention to what is.

Maybe you've noticed:
- **Resistance?** A part of you, perhaps, that doesn't understand why you've chosen to journal.
- **Excitement?** A tingle of anticipation and curiosity at what your writings will reveal.
- **Fear or anxiety?** A feeling of uncertainty about where your thoughts will take you.

Of course, you may have noticed all three – and much more. They're all allowed. This is a place where we can welcome the whole of us, without censorship.

As you move through the prompts, you may hear different parts of you showing up and speaking through your pen. The guidance here is to trust and allow.

Noticing when things feel as if they're getting in the way of the flow – calling it out on the paper, exploring what's happening – can be a beautiful part of the process. Remember, you will only write what feels right for you in the moment. There's no pressure here. No shoulds or musts or oughts. Choosing to write without self-censorship is a generous foundation for Flow Journaling. And just as with any practice, it can take practise.

Mindful Moment
Take a moment to settle now. Get comfortable. You may wish to lie down, lean back or sit as you would when meditating: upright, supported and at ease.

Lean into how your body feels today.

What do you notice? Where might there be some tension? And where is there ease? Simply notice, there's no need to tell yourself the story of that sensation.

And breathe.

Breathe in through your nose and out through your mouth three times. Each time deepening the inhale, extending the exhale. Clearing all the stale air from your lungs, releasing any thoughts from your mind, and coming into a place of peaceful presence.

Allow your breath to return to your normal, relaxed breathing – whatever that feels like today.

Self-Reflection Check-In

What feels useful? What could you pay kind attention to, to inform your journaling practice?

◊

Making your response to resistance part of the practice

◊

Making your response to judgement part of the practice

◊

Making your response to comparison part of the practice

◊

Making deep self-compassion part of the practice

When I am in the flow

How kindness feels

Being present with what challenges me

The gift of *time*

This gift of time, what a generous thing it is to give to ourselves. Yet, we often use lack of time as the reason not to do something – especially if that something is purely for us. Seeing this commitment to journaling as a generous gift for your Self can help cut through some of that internal tension.

How you use your time, and how much you write, depends on you. This book reflects my preferred approach; the way I tend to journal.

I like the freedom of an unlined page. It means sometimes my writing might be BIG and messy (reflecting expansive thinking or tangled thoughts perhaps) and at other times small and neat (reflecting a desire for clarity or more focused thinking perhaps). Noticing how I'm writing can be an interesting reflection on my inner state and help me deepen my reflections on a particular topic. What do you notice?

I tend to write for two pages, but if my journal is big or my writing is small, then that number may change. And while I'm not generally keen on time limits, I see they can be useful too. Even writing for three or four minutes can produce some powerful results. So sometimes I'll play a piece of music that's the length of time I want to journal – something I really enjoy.

For me, playing with different approaches is a lovely way to challenge the part of me that desires consistency and orderliness. Just as having times when I consistently journal every day challenges the part of me that's resistant to rules.

What could be lovely for you to challenge today?

Mindful Moment

Close your eyes, or lower and soften your gaze.

Get comfortable. Sit or lie down, whatever you prefer.

Any distractions – thoughts/sounds/feelings. Perhaps there's the sound of traffic or wind in the trees, or other people's voices as they go about their day. Perhaps there are thoughts of things that have happened in the past – 5 minutes ago, 5 days ago, 5 years ago – or thoughts of what needs to happen in the future – in 5 minutes, 5 days, 5 years. Perhaps there are feelings? Joy, discomfort, anticipation, anxiety, frustration, enthusiasm.

Whatever you notice is okay. As each distraction takes your attention, whisper to yourself, 'This too'.

With this practice, we're allowing everything to be just as it is. Just as when we journal, we allow whatever arises to be present, we're not trying to ignore or stop the thoughts or push away any external sounds or suppress any sensations. We're noticing it all. Everything is allowed to be here, as it is.

This too.

Self-Reflection Check-In

What will most support your own journaling practice?
◇
Allowing whatever arises
◇
Remembering how journaling can help when things feel hard
◇
Noticing any distractions
◇
Remembering this is a practice to enjoy

Giving myself the gift of my attention

Seeing my whole Self through loving eyes

How it is to be sitting here now

Mindful.
Kindful.

What a lot of beautiful words have fallen from your pen (and they are all beautiful, even if some/many/all have felt challenging too). That sense of acceptance, of all that we write, can feel hard to access at times.

Sometimes the words don't flow, so we judge ourselves. And then we feel bad about judging ourselves, so we judge ourselves for judging ourselves. It can get complicated! There are so many ways the inner critic can be activated as we journal, especially if we're exploring things we might ordinarily avoid. The important thing here is to go gently.

Dr Kristin Neff says that self-compassion is treating ourselves as we would treat our dearest friend. And it can be wonderful to experiment with being willing to express the inner judgement – responding to it as though it was being felt by someone you dearly love.

Thinking back to our last Mindful Moment, rather than being self-critical and trying to filter or edit out negative thoughts and feelings, you might choose to write about these too. It's a way of saying that even these are welcome in your journal. We're not trying to suppress or deny any part of our experience... simply noticing and asking how we can bring more compassion here.

Journaling is a place where we can make space for the whole of us. It's a space of belonging. So be kind when you notice something is hard or complex or painful, allow it to surface and show it compassion. I often use terms of endearment towards myself, to help that compassion come through. My darling. My love. Dear heart.

This act of self-compassion can feel the least familiar and the most rewarding aspect of Flow Journaling – the simplicity of being with ourselves, without agenda.

Mindful Moment
Come into a comfortable position. Sit in a chair, feet flat on the floor, arms relaxed by your side or on your knees. Or find a space to sit cross-legged on the floor or a cushion, supporting yourself, upright but not stiff.

Close your eyes and take a few steadying breaths to help settle deeper into where you're sitting.

We're going to practise the 4444 breath. Four breaths – inhaling for a count of four, holding for a count of four, exhaling for a count of four, holding again for a count of four. Go at your own pace, noticing how it feels to be centred in on your breath.

Allow your breath to return to its natural rhythm and pace. And simply notice how it feels to be resting here now.

Notice any sounds – there's no need to follow them or find their source, just notice them drifting by.

Notice any sensations in your body – there's no need to label them, just notice them as they arise.

Notice any thoughts – there's no need to judge them, just notice them as they cycle through.

Now the invitation is to think back to the intention you set at the beginning of this journey.

Is anything else arising? Has that intention deepened, changed, become clearer, stayed the same? A word, a phrase, an image.

Whatever resonates today.

Self-Reflection Check-In

Which of these most resonates with you?

◊

The importance of releasing judgement about how or what you're writing

◊

Practising non-attachment to what you're writing and letting the words go

◊

Bringing more compassion to your writing

◊

Using journaling as a way of staying fully present in the moment

Noticing one small thing with love

What's asking for my attention?

Words of guidance to my younger Self

The still *quiet voice* within

At times when you Flow Journal, you may sense you are reaching a deeper part of yourself.

You might see this as your inner voice, your wisdom, your intuition, your soul, consciousness, your witness, your observer, oneness, your true self, your adult, or as a divine connection – whatever feels most true for you is okay.

I think of mine as compassionate wisdom. The part of me that is connected, creative, reflective and loving. I believe we all hold compassionate wisdom within us. And that when we write, speak, think, feel from this place, the result takes us one step closer to a connected, creative, reflective and loving world.

Eileen Caddy, founder of the Findhorn Foundation, calls it 'the still quiet voice within'. I like this description. It reminds me of my need to be still and quiet in order to listen.

Sometimes my journaling becomes a conversation with this wise part. I find myself asking questions, perhaps in exasperation or in sorrow, and this voice replies. And in the way of wise elders, it doesn't always tell me what I want to hear, but there is always an element of what it says that I find useful to pay attention to.

Having this sense of connection with something deeper within me means I often end my journaling with the words 'thank you'. It may seem such a small thing, but it's become a way of honouring the process, honouring my inner voice, and honouring myself for dedicating the time to do the practice.

I also add a couple of kisses – they slipped from my pen one day and have become a tiny gesture of affection each time I write. How do you thank yourself for this gift of your attention?

Mindful Moment
Notice your posture. Settle. Get comfortable, supported and relaxed. Close your eyes and settle deeper into where you're sitting.

Notice your breath. Notice how it is today. In this moment. How deep or shallow is it? Where do you feel it most? How does your body move with your breath? Is there anything surprising about what you notice? Is everything deeply familiar?

Keep breathing. Keep noticing. Stay with this for a few minutes. And when your mind wanders, as it will, as it does for us all, gently return your attention to your breath.

Now, place your hand on your heart.

And send a message of gratitude to yourself for being here now. Thank yourself for this moment of mindful attention. Thank yourself for taking the time to journal. Thank yourself for this body that holds you here, breathing.

Self-Reflection Check-In

What are you choosing to be grateful for today?
◊
The way you are approaching your journaling
◊
How you're listening to your inner voice
◊
The time you are dedicating to yourself
◊
Your whole Self

Listening to the still quiet voice within

Connection brings me...

Learning to love the whole of me

Full *stop*

When I've reached the end of that day's journaling, I stop. I put my pen down. And I close my book. Most of the time.

Generally I resist the urge to read it through – allowing the words to fall and leaving them where they land. Unless. Unless something so unexpected has arisen that I feel it's useful to take a moment to reflect further on it.

How has it been for you as you've responded to the prompts in this book? Have you re-read or simply closed the book and got on with your day? Either is okay, of course. Some of us may never want to return to what we've written – I know one journaler who writes on a whiteboard and wipes it clean each day. And that's okay too.

I do return to my writing and I often share my journaling – many of my podcast episodes and my books are largely inspired by my journaling practice. But this act of sharing is very much a personal choice.

My feeling is that sometimes it can be useful to return to your writing at a later stage – maybe days, weeks, months or years later… I know many who've found looking back at past journaling created a beautiful opportunity to see what had remained, what had changed, and what they could now attend to more deeply.

Whatever choice you have made as you've gone along, the invitation today is to consider whether this is a useful moment to take stock? To look back at some of what you've written. What do you notice (with love, always with love)?

Mindful Moment
Come into your preferred posture. Close your eyes. Steady and settle your breath.

Today's meditation is created as a space for paying deep attention to how you feel. An open, relaxed, safe space to explore and allow. Emotions, sensations, feelings.

A relaxed awareness of all that is. And when your wonderful, clever mind tries to draw your attention away, simply notice. And whisper to yourself 'thinking'. And return to noticing how you feel.

Emotions, sensations, feelings.

Sink into your body. Allow your body to speak. Listening deeply to all that rises. Not attached, simply aware. Without judgement, without telling the story of that emotion, sensation, feeling.

Simply aware. Relaxed, compassionate and at ease.

Self-Reflection Check-In

Which approach feels preferable for you?
◊
To always look back at what you've written on the day you write it
◊
To experiment with not re-reading your journal on the day you write it
◊
To sometimes return to your writing at a later stage
◊
To never re-read your journal

Looking back I can see

When I let go of expectations

Allowing what is

Creating *rituals*

As you've deepened your journaling practice, what have you noticed about what helps and hinders you?

For me, I know creating a ritual was a large part of what enabled me to build the habit.

Rituals are powerful tools for embedding behaviours. They can include anything and everything – just as with journaling, there are no rules. It's all about observing what you love and building that in. So candles, essential oils, crystals, relaxing music, cushions, comforting blankets, switching off distractions, a warm cup of a nourishing brew, a beautiful book, your favourite pen, lovely lighting. These can all be part of the ritual. All at a time when you're less likely to be disturbed – perhaps telling others you're taking a moment for yourself and asking them to respect that space.

The key is to make your ritual special enough that you feel like you're receiving beautiful attention from yourself, but simple enough that you can easily replicate it.

We can also use journaling in other rituals too. For example, if you're changing an old habit that no longer serves you, releasing an outdated belief, coming to terms with a challenging memory. Marking the shift from then to now by writing it down and then setting it free or welcoming something new can feel powerfully cathartic.

Begin by creating a space that feels special for you, perhaps taking some time to meditate or reflect on what you are releasing and/or receiving. Once you've written everything that needs to be said (mindfully, kindfully), you might choose to (safely) burn the paper you've written on, or perhaps tear it gently into small strips or shapes, whispering your heart's intention.

Mindful Moment
Sit comfortably. Take two or three deep breaths – in through the nose and out through the mouth with a long, slow, sigh.

For a few minutes, feel or imagine the breath moving through the centre of your chest – in the area of your heart.

Metta, or loving kindness, is first practised towards oneself, since we often have difficulty loving others without first loving ourselves. And this is what we'll practise today.

Mentally repeat the following, slowly and steadily:

May I be happy. May I be safe.
May I be healthy. May I live with ease.

As you say each phrase, allow yourself to sink into the intentions they express.

May I be happy. May I be safe.
May I be healthy. May I live with ease.

Loving-kindness meditation consists primarily of connecting to the intention of wishing ourselves and others happiness.

May I be happy. May I be safe.
May I be healthy. May I live with ease.

If you sense feelings of warmth, friendliness, or love arise, connect to them, allowing them to grow as you repeat the phrases.

You might find it helpful to hold an image of yourself in your mind's eye.

Keep repeating the phrases:
May I be happy. May I be safe.
May I be healthy. May I live with ease.

Self-Reflection Check-In

What will you experiment with?
◇
Creating an everyday ritual for journaling
◇
Using journaling to support yourself in releasing stuck feelings and behaviours
◇
Asking, 'How can I bring even more compassion here?'
◇
Practising acceptance that journaling feels better on some days than others

Releasing what no longer serves me

What's helped me make changes?

Creating space for something new

Everything *and* anything

As you've been writing, perhaps you've seen how everything and anything can be used as a topic – we can even journal about journaling itself.

If something is piquing your attention. If a thought has snagged in your brain. If a feeling is persisting in your body. If a word is resonating within you. If an image is showing up strongly. If there's something, however minor, that you're curious about, create a prompt and journal on it.

Beginning with a prompt helps give us a starting point with an open-ended destination. Our brain can focus in on the prompt AND expand out into creative thought.

It can be interesting to take a line from your own journaling and use it to spark new thoughts. Or simply choose a word you love, a phrase you heard someone say, or a line from a favourite piece of poetry or prose.

And for those times when a specific prompt hasn't appeared, it can be useful to have a core prompt, something you can keep returning to again and again.

At those times, I usually begin with, 'Are you there?' with the reply: 'Always, my love'. This opens up my conversation with my compassionate wisdom and always leads somewhere new.

The invitation now is to gather your own inspiration, create your own prompts, and journal on whatever catches your attention. I've included a handful of additional phrases at the back of the book, in case you find these useful.

Mindful Moment
Close your eyes, or lower and soften your gaze. Get comfortable.

As you sit or lie here, notice what you notice.

Let your attention drift.

We're not trying to control anything. Simply noticing any thoughts/sounds/feelings.

Let your attention drift.

And turn your gaze towards something you are grateful for.

Something perhaps that happened in your day. A smile from a stranger. A sip of a warm drink at the perfect temperature. A message of thanks from a friend. Allow a smile of gratitude to begin to grow in your heart and whisper *thank you.*

Cast your mind wider and notice something you are grateful for about a loved one. Someone in your life now, or someone from your past. Feel into a particular memory of them, or the whole of them. Smile upon them in your heart and whisper *thank you.*

Go wider still, and notice the natural world. The warmth of the sun or the cold of the wind on your cheeks. Rain falling softly or heavily from the sky, replenishing the rivers, lakes and seas. Trees moving in the breeze. Green leaves budding, golden leaves falling. The natural cycle of new growth and returning to the earth. Allow that smile of gratitude to grow larger in your heart and whisper th*ank you.*

Self-Reflection Check-In

What are you noticing journaling is helping you with?

◊

It's helping you explore your inner experience

◊

You're creating clarity and calm about things in your internal life

◊

It's helping you explore your external experience

◊

You're creating clarity and calm about things in your external life

My prompt for today

Endings and *beginnings*

Here's an idea I love... everything begins with an ending.

What does this conjure for you?

For me, it brings the image of a bridge. Stepping onto the bridge (ending what was), we cross over the liminal space of change and step into the new beginning of the other side.

It shows us how, as we change, grow, adapt and adopt new habits, behaviours and knowledge, we are in a constant state of flow. Ending and beginning.

◊ What are you noticing is ending and beginning for you here?
◊ How has it been to give yourself this time and compassionate attention?
◊ What's been surprising? Challenging? Exciting? Confusing? Inspiring?
◊ What feels different or the same after you've journaled?
◊ What are you taking and learning from this practice?

As we draw to a close, it might also be useful to reflect on the prompts you used too. Which ones felt like your journaling really flowed? Were there some you chose not to use or changed in some way? Others you'd love to return to? Where could you find future inspiration? Remembering that everything can become part of the practice. We can even use the words of the inner critic as a journaling prompt, and see what your voice of compassionate wisdom has to say. Deepening your self-awareness with profound self-compassion is really what Flow Journaling is all about.

Some additional prompt inspiration...
When I write to myself with love
A gift I'm giving to future me
Opening my mind
Opening my heart
My inner wisdom
The tiny things that hold deep meaning
What's catching my mind's eye
This moment
Only here, only now

Self-Reflection Check-In

What's your final reflection on what you've noticed when you've journaled?

◊

The sense of relief after journaling, as though you've been unburdened

◊

Feeling as though you've found some answers

◊

Finding something feels much clearer to you

◊

Feeling like you've chatted things through with a wise and very dear friend

Everything begins with an ending

About Henny Flynn

Henny lives in Herefordshire, England, with her husband and their dog, Ronnie.

She writes, coaches, speaks and teaches about making and managing deep and lasting change with profound compassion.

You can Journal with Henny through her online gatherings and in person retreats. Connect with her at hennyflynn.co.uk and hear her on the Henny Flynn podcast

hennyflynn.co.uk

Information:

First published:
Inner Work Project, 2024

Text copyright ©
Henny Flynn 2024

All rights reserved.
ISBN 978-1-916563-02-5

Graphic Design:
Supafrank

Printed in the UK by Pureprint.

Discover more workbooks to put your good intentions into daily practice.

www.innerworkproject.com